THE MONEY MAZE
THE CHRISTIAN AND MONEY

THE MONEY MAZE
THE CHRISTIAN AND MONEY

Stephen Baker

40 Beansburn, Kilmarnock, Scotland

ISBN-13: 978 1 914273 12 4

Published with kind permission from Emmaus Bible College

Copyright © 2021 by John Ritchie Ltd.
40 Beansburn, Kilmarnock, Scotland

www.ritchiechristianmedia.co.uk

All rights reserved. No part of this publication may be reproduced, stored in a retrievable system, or transmitted in any form or by any other means – electronic, mechanical, photocopy, recording or otherwise – without prior permission of the copyright owner.

Typeset by John Ritchie Ltd., Kilmarnock
Printed by Bell & Bain Ltd., Glasgow

CONTENTS

Background and Reason for Writing 7

Index and Outline 9

1. The History of Money 13

2. Money as a Means to an End 19

3. Saving for a Rainy Day 25

4. Supporting or Propping Up 29

5. A Roof Over Your Head 33

6. Easy Access Credit 39

7. Getting What You Want or Need - Spending Money 47

8. Giving to God, His Work and His Workers 53

9. The Piggy Bank is Empty - Budgeting and Planning 61

10. Insuring the Future - Wise or Overkill? 65

11. Ending Well - Planning for Retirement 69

Concluding Comments 73

THE MONEY MAZE

BACKGROUND AND REASON FOR WRITING

Money has a strange effect on people. For some people, accumulating money and creating wealth is a habit and the aim of their life is to ensure that they are never without it. Others view money as a means to an end - it's a necessary evil but in itself it has no value - its only purpose is to help them get through life with as little hassle as possible. There are people who consider money as evil in itself as it brings out the raw sinful responses of greed, avarice, covetousness, jealousy etc. At the opposite end of the spectrum there are those who see money as a positive thing, to be desired and a visible evidence of success, skill, creativity, and intelligence. This book will explore the truth about what money is and look at it from a biblical perspective; in other words - What does the Bible say about money?

Exploring money matters is a bit like a maze. I can't be sure where I will end up and how long it will take to find the right answers, but please stay with me as I talk to you about the various topics. You might be reading this book purely as a reference book and so you will want to skip certain chapters and get straight to the section that interests you or answers your current question. Why do some people feel forced to borrow money and why do others borrow willingly so that they can have the latest and best? The question is, is it right to borrow in any circumstances? What about lending to your family or your friends? Is it a case of right and wrong or do we just need a good dose of wisdom?

We all need a place to live so should you rent rather than mortgage? Do you borrow the maximum or make a modest purchase? My aim is to research scripture and hopefully give you a helpful insight into what the Bible says. However, I might have opinions and advice that you don't agree with, so bear with me. You'll need to do your homework and check the advice against the Bible and make your own decision.

So finally, a little bit about me. My name is Stephen Baker. For just over twenty-nine years I worked in the world of business. Twenty-seven of those years were spent working for a British Bank (Scottish to be precise. If you've heard of canny Scots, you'll know that banking and finance are in their DNA) and so I am familiar with the world of money and what a lack of it or a surplus of it can do to a person's behaviour. Greed is a terrible force for evil and poverty and the need to survive can have an equally devastating effect on a person's life. For two years after leaving banking, I worked with a Christian colleague helping business owners who were struggling with their businesses. Today, I am in the privileged position of serving God in a full-time capacity. The years have passed very quickly, and I am privileged to have a lovely wife, two adult children (plus a son-in-law and a daughter-in-law) and two grandchildren. Enough of me, let's outline where we are going in 'The Money Maze'.

INDEX AND OUTLINE

Chapter 1 - *The History of Money, Hard Work and Earning*

Where did money come from? How did money develop? - through barter, cash, banks, credit cards and electronic payments. What does the Bible say about how we earn money? Should we have a work ethic, sometimes called a 'Protestant work ethic'? How much work is too much work and are there any jobs that are unsuitable for a believer?

Chapter 2 - *Money as a means to an end - What drives you in life? - The love of money!*

What is money meant to be used for? Is it good or evil in itself? Why can money be the cause of family feuds, business fallouts, national crises, and divorce? Can it be used for good as well as evil? What about tax avoidance/evasion or Gift Aid?

Chapter 3 - *Saving for a rainy day*

What should my attitude to saving be? How does the Lord's return impact on my savings goals? Should we accept interest on savings in light of the Bible's teaching on usury?

Chapter 4 - *Supporting or Propping up - Being a Guarantor*

Is it wrong to be a guarantor? What are the implications and the pitfalls? When or why would you become a guarantor for someone?

Chapter 5 - *A roof over your head - Mortgaging, Renting or Lodging*

Is getting a mortgage to buy a house just the same as renting? Is it more prudent to buy, and have some long-term value in the building, than to spend years paying rent and ending up with nothing?

Chapter 6 - *Quick Returns and Easy access credit - Gambling and Debt*

As credit is readily available - should we use it? Is it wiser to save and spend rather than use credit and pay back later? Is the use of credit facilities just part of modern life or is a symptom of a covetous society? Is borrowing outlawed in the Bible? Should you lend to relatives and friends and should you charge them interest? What are reasonable reasons for borrowing? What does the Bible have to say about gambling - lottery, the bottle tombola at the school fair, raffle tickets for charity etc? Is direct share ownership gambling?

Chapter 7 - *Getting what you want or need - Spending money*

What does the Bible have to say about spending money - on ourselves, on our children etc.? To what extent can a believer have a clear conscience about enjoying the ordinary things of life? Can money fuel our greed and does waiting help us trust in God more and develop patience?

Chapter 8 - *Giving to God*

What are my obligations to God when it comes to money? Should a Christian tithe? How do I decide what to give the Lord? How do I decide what to give my money to and are there trustworthy routes I can use? Should I only give to the Lord or do I have a role in social justice?

Chapter 9 - *The piggy bank is empty - budgeting and planning*

Do I need to do some money planning? What's left after all my essential expenses are covered? How should I plan for my purchases?

Chapter 10 - *Insuring the future - wise or overkill?*

Should a believer use insurance? Is it wise to provide for your family upon your unexpected decease?

Chapter 11 - *Ending well - Planning for Retirement*

Should I plan for retirement and ensure a happy ending? Is this prudent or does it show a lack of faith? What about saving for the end days of life - is this wise or presumptuous? The years will fly by so how do you plan for the years when you are unable to earn? Is it wise to write a will?

Concluding Comments & Summary

How do I value money and its use? Society often rates people according to the size of their house, car etc. How does a Christian avoid these pitfalls? Does the prosperity gospel and similar beliefs have an impact on how we think about money and success?

So, what have you learned from this book? How can you change the way you think and help others to do the same?

THE MONEY MAZE

CHAPTER 1
THE HISTORY OF MONEY

> *'Money is only a tool. It will take you wherever you wish, but it will not replace you as the driver.'* Ayn Rand, Writer and Philosopher

> *'For even when we were with you, this we commanded you, that if any would not work, neither should he eat.'* 2 Thessalonians 3. 10

I don't consider myself to be old, but I would have to admit that in my lifetime the word 'money' has come to mean a lot more things than it meant in my youth. In our current culture, as people go about their business, they don't need to carry cash in their pocket. Coins have become a bit of a nuisance and even cards that until recently were thought to be a fairly modern means of payment are rapidly being replaced by payment systems on phones.

There are many new terms that are banded about and need to be defined unless you are familiar with them. For instance, if I asked you how you use a 'bitcoin' I wonder if you would know what I meant. A bitcoin is a digital virtual currency which was created in 2009 and that uses peer-to-peer technology to facilitate instant payments. I am told it follows the ideas set out in a white paper by the mysterious Satoshi Nakamoto, whose identity has still to be verified. Do you know what a trip to a currency exchange or a digital currency exchange is? That is not for discussion in this book, but it just serves to illustrate the complexity of the world of finance and money that we currently live in.

This book is essentially about what the Bible has to say about money. The aim is to help the Christian believer develop habits and practices, from a biblical perspective, so that money becomes less of a master and more of a servant enabling us to live efficiently in the 21st century.

What is money?

The early references to money in the Bible teach us a lot about its function. Before I give you a quick overview of these references, let's talk about money in general terms. Money is a commodity that is used as a medium of exchange. In and of itself, it is nothing. It could be a shell, a metal coin, a rock, or a piece of paper with an image on it. Money is only as valuable as people deem it to be. It has got nothing to do with the physical value of the item, but it has been given value and is treated as a medium of exchange. It is also used as a unit of measurement and can be the means of storing wealth. These definitions in themselves should teach us that money is really of little significance. It only becomes of value because human beings have deemed it to be so. It should not be surprising, then, that the New Testament teaches that the problem with money is not in the commodity but in the love that people have for it. When Paul writes to Timothy in 1 Timothy chapter 6 verse 10, he makes a statement which has often been misquoted. Paul says, 'For the love of money is the root of all evil'. This statement will be referred to many times in this book, I have no doubt, but it would be worthwhile at this stage to point out that the passage is highlighting the dangers of the passionate driving force of greed. We are taught in verse 8 to be content with food and clothing, necessities that we in my country often take for granted. In this section we are reminded that we came into the world with nothing and it is absolutely certain that we can't take anything with us when we leave. In light of this we are being taught to be content. This should be one of the wonderful characteristics of a genuine believer in Jesus Christ. For them, life is not built around what we have and what we have gained but the solid foundation of life is the value that we have been given as a human being and the added joy of being saved by God's grace.

Early references in the Bible to money

In Genesis chapter 13 we learned Abraham was very rich in cattle, in silver, and in gold. What a person owns and the money a person has in the bank has always been indicative of their wealth. Now we know, as Christians, that real wealth is not measured in personal assets but in the blessings we have from God, Eph. 1. 7, 18, Rev 2. 9. So, as we develop this subject please do not lose sight of these riches. The money you have is only for this life, but it can be used for the kingdom of God, Luke 16. 9-12. However, money itself will have no significance in the next life.

Genesis chapter 23 verse 16 highlights the fact that money was being used as a medium of exchange many thousands of years ago. Abraham had to weigh out the money (hence our expression - 'worth his weight in gold') when he was making payment for the field he was purchasing to bury his beloved wife. Not much has changed - money still changes hands when a transaction takes place and, sadly, we still need to deal with the practicalities of paying for things while handling bereavement and sadness.

When you read the story of Joseph in chapters 37-50 you will see regular references to money. Joseph was sold for twenty pieces of silver in chapter 37, the brothers needed money to buy food supplies when they visited Egypt in the days of famine and Joseph in his 'Saviour' role bartered with the Egyptians for their money and land in exchange for food. 'Money makes the world go round' - well, it certainly plays a major part in enabling people to eat, live and get on with their daily lives.

So, we need money and you don't get it without working for it, so what should a believer's attitude be to earning money?

The Principle of working to earn money

First of all, we must recognize that the principle of work existed before sin came into the world. The six-day process of creation is described by God as 'his work', Gen. 2. 2. He enjoyed it and the result was good. On day six, He said it was very good, 1. 31. Adam was commissioned by God to work in the Garden of Eden. He was instructed to 'dress it and to keep it,' 2. 15. So, we learn from this that work is not bad in itself. Many of us have found work difficult and tiresome but that is because when sin came into the world work took on a whole different meaning. One of the results of sin was that for Adam to put 'food on the table' he was going to have to sweat, 3. 19. Work was going to be hard going, tough and difficult at times. Now, unless you live in a developing country you, like me, probably haven't experienced work in that sense. However, our grandparents did. Most of them worked the land, fished the sea, mined the earth, and did hard to work to provide for their families and there was nothing wrong with that. In fact, scripture makes it very clear that providing for your family is a vital part of being a believer, 1 Tim. 5. 8, and to do less than that is to deny the faith. In another passage Paul writes: 'For even when we were with you, this we

Save and spend rather than borrow and pay back."

commanded you, that if any would not work, neither should he eat,' 2 Thess. 3. 10. So work is honouring to God, we need to provide for our families, the work ethic was introduced by God and we are denying what we believe if we don't act responsibly and work hard.

Working should not take up all our time

So how are you going to make enough money to pay for everything or as we say, 'to make ends meet'. Here are a few general principles that will help us.

1. You don't need everything immediately.

2. You don't need things just because other people have them.

3. Live within what you earn and not what you wish you earned.

4. Save and spend rather than borrow and pay back.

These statements can all backed up from scripture. I'll leave you with a couple and then as we move into the following chapters some of the rationale behind the principles will become clearer.

'And having food and clothing, with these we shall be content,' 1 Timothy 6. 8, NKJV.

'Let your conduct be without covetousness; be content with such things as you have. For He Himself has said, "*I will never leave you nor forsake you,*"' Hebrews 13. 5, NKJV.

'Set your mind on things above, not on things on the earth,' Colossians 3. 2, NKJV.

In light of this, I think you will agree that, if possible, you should control your working hours so that you can be involved in church activities and serving God, to spend time with family and to make sure that focus is not just on money and things. Does that mean there are certain jobs that you should not do - it could! You would need to decide before God whether any specific job is out of bounds for you - from a scriptural perspective i.e., is it wrong to be involved in that occupation and from a personal time management perspective - will it take my focus off the most important things in my life?

As you can see, this is a big subject and one that touches many aspects of our lives. My prayer is that the Lord will help you (and me) to make good choices in light of what is pleasing and glorifying to Him.

Don't leave us now, grab a coffee and keep reading.

CHAPTER 2
MONEY AS A MEANS TO AN END

> *'Everyone should get rich, and famous, and get everything they ever dreamed of; so that they can see that's not the answer.' Jim Carrey, Comedian*

> *'For the love of money is the root of all evil: which while some coveted after, they have erred from the faith, and pierced themselves through with many sorrows.' 1 Timothy 6. 10*

So, what is money meant to be used for? Is it just a method by which we make payments, a means of trading and purchasing, or is it in itself something to be accumulated, treasured, and used to demonstrate how successful we are in life? This latter definition appears to be one that is commonly held but whether you accept it depends on what drives you in life.

Money initially was developed as a method by which things could be acquired and exchanges made. This meant that one person could exchange their goods for someone else's - this was called barter. We probably all accept that money as a method of purchasing and selling and as a means for acquiring things is a valid concept. However, the question we want to address is - is money essentially evil? In other words, does money have any inherent qualities, is it good or bad? Why is it the cause of so many family feuds or business fallouts? Divorces take place because of money and marriages can be under pressure because of strained finances. At times, nations struggle with their economies and critical situations arise because of money. Having said all that, we also know that money can bring about good. Gift Aid exists in the same world as tax avoidance or evasion. Money can be used for charitable purposes as well as to fund drug addiction. So, money in itself isn't good or bad – it's what we do with it that makes the difference. These are the types of issues that we wish to address in this chapter.

Let's think of some general principles about human nature as this will help us understand why money can become a catalyst for both good and evil. The first statement I want you to think about is found in the book of Jeremiah chapter 17 verse 9. It states that 'the heart is deceitful above all things, and desperately wicked'. First, we discover that we have the capacity to deceive ourselves. The rest of the verse reminds us that we are not always aware of how harmful that deceit is - 'who can know it?' We need to be aware of this when we are dealing with money. The verse I quoted at the beginning of the chapter reminds me that it is 'the love of money' that is the root of all evil. That is, there are desires in my heart that produce actions and behaviours that are evil and wrong. The Lord Jesus expanded on this idea in Mark chapter 7 when He described what comes out of the human heart. He tells His audience that it is not the physical uncleanness of the world that they should be worried about but the filth that comes out of a person. That is what really defiles them. The list is very sobering. It is a lesson about the extreme behaviour that humans are capable of. The list includes theft, greed, deceit, and envy - all behaviours that could have an impact on how we handle money. No wonder we make such a mess of the world when our desires are rooted in

> **Money can produce dirty habits and desires."**

an evil character. It is not a surprising, therefore, that money becomes a great temptation and a great resource for evil if these desires are not properly understood and controlled.

The other thing I noticed when reading the Bible is that it doesn't seem to matter who you are - you can still get into bad habits and let money rule your life instead of it being your servant. In 1st Timothy chapter 3 when Paul is teaching Timothy about 'church life' he says in verse 3 that elders should not be 'greedy of filthy lucre' and he gives the same warning in verse 8 about deacons. I know that the King James translation of this verse is quite quaint, but I do think that it makes the point effectively. Money can produce dirty habits and desires; it can create indecent motives and cravings and it can make a person so eager to gain that they ignore how much it degrades their character in the process. This is written about elders and deacons who are meant to be mature, wise leaders of local churches and so the warning should be heeded by all of us.

In contrast to this, I was delighted when I read Psalm 19 and discovered that the writer valued the Word of God so much that he felt that it worth more than gold - 'They are more precious than gold, than much pure gold,' Psalm 19. 10, NIV. I wonder how much value you and I put on the Word of God. In comparison to the world's investments and wealth, is it priceless to me?

Let's look for a moment at the positive ways in which we can use money. We will look at this in more detail in chapter 8, but I want to start you thinking about it in this chapter.

The Apostle Paul advises, Timothy, a younger man, in 1st Timothy chapter 6 verses 17-19. His advice is about rich people, but in world terms most people living in Europe and the United States would be classified as rich - we have homes, food, clothes, phones, transport and lots more. In this passage, Paul says - 'Charge them that are rich in this world, that they be not highminded, nor trust in uncertain riches, but in the living God, who giveth us richly all things to enjoy; That they do good, that they be rich in good works, ready to distribute, willing to communicate; Laying up in store for themselves a good foundation against the time to come, that they may lay hold on eternal life'.

The main lessons I learned from this passage are:

1. Don't depend on your money or be proud about what you have.

2. Remember wealth is uncertain and unpredictable.

3. Trust in God not money.

4. God is the source of all the things you enjoy, and He is very generous.

5. Use what you have for the benefit of others.

6. Do your sharing and charitable acts willingly.

7. Charitable giving is an investment for the future - God measures your generosity in terms of what you give, what you have left and why you give. Other passages of the Bible, such as Mark 12.44, also make this clear.

The Hebrew letter says a similar thing in chapter 13 verse 16 - 'But to do good and to communicate forget not: for with such sacrifices God is well pleased'.

We also learn in 2nd Corinthians chapter 9 verse 7 that cheerful giving makes God really happy.

So what can we learn from these two scriptures:

1. To give generously.

2. Giving makes God happy.

3. Our giving is a spiritual investment.

What methods should we use to give?

I think that our primary responsibility is to give through a local church as God has entrusted trustworthy men in the church with the responsibility of handling money. Acts chapter 6 and 2 Corinthians chapters 8 and 9 teach and illustrate this principle.

It would also be wise and prudent to give using the best mechanisms that your country or society legally permits. So in the UK this would be using Gift Aid, through registered charities and organizations that have government approval to handle funds. These methods are both legal and cost effective. This is important both in terms of obeying the law of the land and being wise in the use of our money.

So do remember that God loves a 'cheerful giver' but only give as God has prospered you. But more of that later. Time for another short break!

THE MONEY MAZE

CHAPTER 3
SAVING FOR A RAINY DAY

▎ *'Saving for a rainy day.' - A. F. Grazzini*

▎ *'Store up for yourselves treasures in heaven.' Matthew 6. 20, NASB*

You might have heard the expression 'saving for a rainy day'. Its origin can be traced back to the mid-1500s. It is found in an Italian play written by A. F. Grazzini called 'La Spiritata'. The idea of the 'rainy day' is that there will be times when things are difficult, when there are clouds in the sky and the future doesn't look so good. So, the advice is, that you should set aside something you can afford to save, until a real need arises.

This raises a couple of things we need to think about. What if you are living hand to mouth and have nothing to spare? I think the answer is obvious, you can't save what you don't have, so don't try. It's the same principle (in reverse) that we ended chapter two with - you can't give what you don't have. But remember that sacrificing a few pleasures today so that you will have food on the table tomorrow is worthwhile doing.

There are other basic principles that come to mind as I write this. I will note them now in case I forget to deal with them later.

You may need to develop them in your own mind. They are:

1. Always live within your means.

2. Don't spend what you don't have.

3. Make sacrifices to help others - see 2 Corinthians 8. 2,3.

4. You don't need to have the same as everyone else.

5. Be satisfied and content with what you have - Hebrews 13. 5.

But, back to the principle of saving.

In the Old Testament God describes His people, Israel, as saving in a negative sense. In effect He warns them about saving the wrong things. All of their evil behaviour and words were storing up God's judgment against them, Deut. 32. 34. This might be an abstract idea, but it illustrates the fact that people have been saving for generations.

The Lord Jesus talks about saving in Matthew chapter 6 verses 19-21 - 'Do not store up for yourselves treasures on earth, where moth and rust destroy, and where thieves break in and steal. But store up for yourselves treasures in heaven, where neither moth nor rust destroys, and where thieves do not break in or steal; for where your treasure is, there your heart will be also,' NASB.

There are a number of lessons that I learn from the words of the Lord Jesus.

1. What I treasure most I will love.

2. Earthly wealth will not last forever.

3. Earthly investments can be stolen or lose value rapidly.

4. There is an investment that is deflation proof, cannot be stolen and will make me focus on the right things in life.

The other passage I want you to think about is one that we have already mentioned in Chapter 2. In 1 Timothy chapter 6 verses 18, 19 Paul writes, 'Instruct them to do good, to be rich in good works, to be generous and ready to share, storing up for themselves the treasure of a good foundation for the future, so that they may take hold of that which is life indeed,' NASB.

We must pay attention to what is being taught here. Cash, bonds, and savings are not the only thing that we can invest in. Good works for the Christian produces wealth that is of lasting value. Generosity and sharing what we have is better than keeping all of our wealth to indulge ourselves. Using your money for the good of others is a wise investment in God's eyes.

Let me summarize the advice that scripture gives us in this area.

It is essential to provide for your family, 1 Tim. 5. 8, so if that means you need to save up to pay for things, that is the proper thing to do. We will deal with the question of borrowing in another chapter.

If your aim is to build up large reserves of money to feel wealthy, then that is wrong and the advice of the Lord Jesus and the Apostle Paul is to invest in heaven's wealth.

The fact that the Lord is coming back should not affect whether we save or not. On the same basis that we need to work for a living but still live expecting the Lord Jesus to return tomorrow so we will save when appropriate, 2 Thess. 3. 10, 12.

The question of interest on savings is one that needs to be considered carefully. The simple answer is that it is acceptable to receive interest when it is part of a legal transaction and it is not disadvantaging an individual in the process. The Old Testament usury laws were written to protect individuals, Deut. 23. 19, 20, not to prevent profit being made on transactions. In the New Testament making profit is not condemned but is clearly seen as normal. For instance, in James chapter 4 verse 13 the man being described buys and sells with the aim of making profit. Interest on investments and savings is nothing more than making profit on the use of the resource of money. The Lord Jesus in one of His parables, Luke chapter 19 verse 23, talks about the option of putting money in the Bank and earning interest on the funds.

Invest with interest in the right commodities!

CHAPTER 4
SUPPORTING OR PROPPING UP

> *'Don't be one of those who enter agreements, who put up security for loans. If you have nothing with which to pay, even your bed will be taken from under you.' - King Solomon*

> *'Deliver yourself like a gazelle from the hunter's hand.'* **Proverbs 6. 5, NASB**

Before we start this chapter be aware that we will discuss in Chapter 6 whether a Christian should be borrowing at all and in Chapter 7 about living beyond our means.

Let me paint a picture for you and then I will seek to answer the questions it raises. Imagine you are applying for a business loan and don't have enough security to offer to satisfy the lender. For those of you who have never been in this situation, let me explain. When you ask a bank or a financial institution to lend you money, they will normally look at a number of things:

1. How much you want to borrow?

2. What you need it for?

3. How long will it take you to repay the loan?

4. What is your monthly income and expenditure and what funds do you have to meet the monthly repayments?

And finally ...

5. Do you have anything to offer the bank that they could use to repay the loan if you fail to meet the repayments?

The conditions will be different depending on what type of loan you are arranging. For smaller amounts you may get an unsecured loan but for larger purchases such as cars, houses, working capital for a business or to purchase a business asset you will be required to give something as security. So, for example, a Hire Purchase Agreement is signed on the basis that the car belongs to the finance company until you have repaid the loan. A mortgage to buy a property, we will deal with this in detail in Chapter 5, is given on the basis that the lender has the right to sell your home, within certain legal rules, if you default on your mortgage payment.

However, sometimes you might not be able to give the appropriate security and the lender will ask you if someone will guarantee the loan on your behalf. So, here is the question - as a Christian, is it a good idea to be a guarantor for someone else?

Here are a couple of passages on this topic from the scriptures. Read them, mull them over in your mind and we will then discuss them.

> *Proverbs 6. 1-7*
> *'My son, if you have become surety for your neighbour, have given a pledge for a stranger, if you have been snared with the words of your mouth, have been caught with the words of your mouth, do this then, my son, and*

> *deliver yourself; since you have come into the hand of your neighbour, go, humble yourself, and importune your neighbour. Give no sleep to your eyes, nor slumber to your eyelids; deliver yourself like a gazelle from the hunter's hand and like a bird from the hand of the fowler. Go to the ant, O sluggard, observe her ways and be wise, which, having no chief, Officer or ruler, prepares her food in the summer and gathers her provision in the harvest. How long will you lie down, O sluggard? When will you arise from your sleep?' NASB.*

Excuse the long quote but I have included all of it as I think that the Holy Spirit through Solomon is teaching a very clear lesson from nature.

1. Your words have trapped you if you become a guarantor.

2. If you have done this get out of it as soon as you can even if you need to 'eat humble pie' in the process. Don't sleep on it, act quickly.

3. Solomon then reminds us, from the world of the hunter, of the dangers of being trapped and the wisdom of the ant in preparing food for winter. If animals can see the danger of being trapped and the wisdom of being prepared, then so should we.

> ***Proverbs 11. 15***
> *'He who is guarantor for a stranger will surely suffer for it, but he who hates being a guarantor is secure.' NASB.*

This is a clear statement. You will suffer if you become a guarantor but avoiding it is a secure position to take.

> *Proverbs 17. 18*
> *'One without sense enters an agreement and puts up security for his friend.' CSB.*

Note the blunt message - you are acting foolishly, without sense, if you put up security for a friend.

> *Proverbs 22. 26-27*
> *'Don't be one of those who enter agreements, who put up security for loans. If you have nothing with which to pay, even your bed will be taken from under you.' CSB.*

The final lesson from the Proverbs on this issue is that the danger of losing is very real if you become a guarantor. Today, in the UK, all credit agreements legally must state clearly that any security offered could be used. In other words, the danger of losing what you have is very real - Solomon says it could be your bed - we would say: 'You could lose the roof over your head'.

The Apologetics Study Bible says: 'Becoming responsible for someone else's debt is the epitome of folly because the person does not know how much such a commitment may cost him. Given the serious risk that this involves, Proverbs exhorts the person who has made this mistake to do whatever he can to extricate himself from the unwise commitment. It is unlikely that Proverbs means this as an absolute prohibition against ever cosigning for another person's loan, but given the risks, it should always be entered into with extreme care'.

I think that is great advice and summarizes what we have learned about this topic.

CHAPTER 5
A ROOF OVER YOUR HEAD

> *'An Englishman's home is his castle.'* Sir Edward Coke

> *'Jacob was a quiet man who stayed at home.'* Genesis 25:27, CSB

A Home

Home is a wonderful place! I love my home and all that I associate with it - the relaxed atmosphere, the sense of belonging, the security of being in a safe place, its privacy, the warm love, and fun-soaked atmosphere. I could go on.

I appreciate that for many people home is not always like this but thankfully it is for many and it is what God desires for everyone. I once came across a lovely verse in the Psalms which said that God 'sets the solitary in families,' Psalm 68. 6, NKJV. Some translations say that 'God makes a home for the lonely,' NASB, but whatever translation you read you come away with the strong impression that God created families for the social good of mankind. He doesn't like us to be lonely and, in fact, one of the first things that He did after creating Adam, the first man, was to provide a wife for him so that he would not be alone.

A home, of course, is more than a house but this whole idea of marriage and family relationships focuses your mind on finding a place to live. Traditionally, people lived with their families until they were married and then they established their own home or household. Many people now leave home while they are single, long before they marry and for some marriage is not the pathway that God takes them down in life.

Rent or Buy

Whether you are setting up a home as a single person or planning to marry and find a home, the question of whether to buy or rent must be considered. Is it wiser and more prudent to take out a mortgage and eventually own a property or would it be better to rent?

Your personal answers to these questions will be influenced by many factors. We are going to consider some of them but try to focus on what the Bible would say to help us make the right choice.

Let me outline some of the things that might influence your thinking on this issue:

1. Your family background - did your parents rent, mortgage, or buy?

2. The area you were brought up in and the thinking of your peer group.

3. Your job and need to be able to move quickly to another area for a job.

4. Your financial situation and how you think your career will progress.

> **... within its pages [the Bible] are principles that we can apply to all the circumstances of life."**

5. The nation you live in and the national attitude to buying or renting.

6. The type of property that is available where you live or would like to live.

7. The availability and affordability of loans for property.

8. The market value of property in your area and what you could afford.

As you can see from my list, and you might have more to add to the list, there is a lot to consider when thinking about where to live.

First of all, I want to start by thinking about what the Bible says, in principle, about this issue. Do bear in mind that the Bible was not written to give you a specific answer to every question you have but within its pages are principles that we can apply to all the circumstances of life. It is a book of wisdom and we would be wise to follow the guidance that it gives for our lives.

Is it a waste of money to rent a property?

For as long as you rent a house, you will never own it. One way of thinking about this is that, as a Christian, you are not meant to build treasures on earth, Matthew 6. 19, and so to own a home goes against this principle. The alternative view would be that as a believer you have a responsibility to be a wise steward of the resources that God has given you, Matthew 25. 14-30, Luke

16. 1-12, and to rent is to pour your resources into something but end up with nothing at the end of the day. Do bear in mind that the house is not yours until it is paid for and mortgaging is effectively renting from the lender. If you can save for the appropriate deposit and can afford the monthly repayments this would be the most prudent way to go. Having said that, let me warn you:

- A. Do not borrow more than you can afford in terms of monthly repayments.

- B. Borrowing may be impossible for some people.

- C. Be content once you have made a decision.

- D. Do not buy a house as an investment but as a home.

- E. Whatever choice you make have an open home, Hebrews 13. 2, and use your home for the glory of God, Col. 3. 17.

- F. If you buy or rent do not become too attached to your home.

This chapter is not meant to give financial advice or to push you into borrowing. All of your choices have to be made in light of the Word of God, your personal financial circumstances and after taking advice from people who are qualified to give you financial advice.

Getting into Debt

While the Bible prohibits a Christian from being in debt to individuals, Romans 13. 8, and demands that a believer pays their taxes and civic dues, Romans 13. 6, 7, it does not forbid formal borrowing from a financial institution.

The legal arrangements that sit behind any form of formal borrowing mean that as long as you keep up your repayments you are not in debt to them. The agreement states that you are repaying a set amount of money plus interest over a fixed period. It is a transaction from which you and the lender benefit. No one should be disadvantaged which is the key when debt is being discussed in scripture. Plus, as I indicated earlier, the fact that the lender effectively owns the property until full repayment has been made means that legally you are not 'in debt' to the organization.

At the end of the day whether you rent or borrow will depend on:

1. The factors described in this chapter.

2. Your conscience and conviction before God.

3. The situation that God has brought you into in your life.

Having said all that please learn to be content with what you have, Hebrews 13. 5, make plans and include the Lord in the decision, James 4. 15. Please don't hanker after bigger and better things, Col. 3.5 and make sure that you have peace in your heart about any decisions that you make and be thankful, Col. 3. 15.

Happy house hunting!

THE MONEY MAZE

CHAPTER 6
EASY ACCESS CREDIT

> 'The rich ruleth over the poor, and the borrower is servant to the lender.' Proverbs 22:7

> 'All of these motives are wrong for the Christian, for they are all self-centered and materialistic.' Billy Graham

There are a lot of issues raised in the outline for this chapter but what I want to do is think about what the Bible teaches about borrowing in principle and then I will address the other questions.

If you have read the 'Background and Reason for Writing' at the beginning of this book you will be aware that I spent many years working in a bank. However, I am not writing to justify the fact that I loaned money to people over those years. I do not think that the Bible teaches that lending money is unscriptural or unethical, but I do believe that there is a right way to lend and conditions of lending should be ethical and biblical.

Does the Bible forbid borrowing?

The simple answer to that is: No. It does not directly condemn lending, nor does it infer that it is wrong, but it does gives clear warnings about the lender/borrower relationship.

In Proverbs chapter 22 verse 7 we read 'The rich ruleth over the poor, and the borrower is servant to the lender'. This is a very clear statement, warning of the severity of the debt relationship that exists when someone is borrowing. They become obligated to the person that they are borrowing from. Be careful, this is serious!

One of the interesting things to look at in scripture is the incidental references to various topics. I don't mean that there is anything incidental or insignificant in scripture but that in some passages reference is made to someone or something that is not the main topic of the passage. The reference however is enlightening. For instance, in Matthew chapter 25 verse 27, the Lord Jesus refers to the bank or the money changers and the payment of interest. In Matthew chapter 5 verse 42 he talks about lending and not refusing to lend and in Luke chapter 6 verse 35 the Lord Jesus talks about lending to your enemies and not looking for a return on your money. These asides make it clear that lending and depositing with the money changers or banks was a normal part of life.

In Psalm chapter 37 verse 21 we read these words: 'The wicked borrows and does not repay, but the righteous shows mercy and gives,' NKJV. It is clear that the problem here is not the fact that a person borrows but the wickedness is in the fact that a person borrows and does not pay back. Of course, the opposite is so true, that the righteous person should aim to be a giver and not a borrower. The principle of borrowing is not condemned but the injustice of failing to repay the loan is. A believer should borrow wisely and make sure that they have the ability to repay the loan on the agreed terms. They should think and look carefully at their income and expenditure before borrowing.

In summary, the Bible does not teach that borrowing is a sin. It does discourage getting into debt and plainly warns against its practical and spiritual dangers. The instruction to the believer is that we should be wise in the way we manage our finances. My advice is if you can avoid debt then do so. But if you must take a loan, do it wisely with a secure repayment plan, paying it off as quickly as you are able to.

Save and Spend or Borrow and Repay

People in the 21st century have been pre-conditioned to think that if they want something, they should be able to get it straight away. People who design loan facilities, credit card systems and payment systems play to this way of thinking. They understand the drivers that make us greedy and covetous and so they make it very easy to get things straight away and pay for them later or over an extended period of time. A wise way to live is to save and then spend. Saving money is a good discipline and it makes you think hard before you part with your hard-earned cash (I know that it is an old-fashioned expression, but I like the sound of it). A good principle to work on is only to borrow for things that are of long-term value, such as a car or a home. You should save, and spend the money when you have it, for things that only have a short life span that you will need to replace regularly.

If you decide to borrow, think carefully about which of the sophisticated methods of borrowing you use. Do your research and calculate what is the most cost-effective way of borrowing. As we now live in a competitive world, where there are a wide range of options such as Hire Purchase and PCP, you have a lot of things to consider. As a believer you should be a good steward of your money and so you need to shop around, work out the figures and choose wisely how you will spend your money.

Payment Systems

In the cashless society most people use cards or phones to make payments. Payments through phone apps such as 'PayPal' or 'MoneyGram' are commonplace and extremely easy to use, therefore we all need to be careful. Credit cards and the equivalent can be used effectively to manage your expenditure. But a note of warning. Both cashless payments out of your bank account (a debit card) and cashless payments from a credit card mean that you can spend money without being aware of what you have left in your account or what the statement balance will be at the end of the month. You need to be careful using these methods of payment, so you don't run up a debt you didn't intend to. Banks and financial institutions are all too willing to lend but you are the one who has to repay what you borrow at the end of the day. If you monitor what you spend on paper or on a phone app, you will be able to manage your finances quite effectively. Be aware that if you don't clear your balance on a Credit Card you will normally pay either a fee or interest. So, check the terms and conditions and know what you will be charged before you use these services. It's your responsibility to be a good steward of the Lord's money!

Lending to friends and family

We have already discussed in Chapter 4 about the dangers of being a guarantor. There are as many difficult issues to handle when lending to friends as in vouching to support their borrowing. It is interesting to note that Jews were not permitted to charge interest when they loaned money or goods to their brothers, but it was permissible to charge interest to non-Jews, Deut. 23. 19, 20. The amazing promise is that God would bless the Jew in their land and that they did not need to make a profit by charging each other interest. The blessing of

"'God loveth a cheerful giver' 2 Corinthians 9:7."

giving is also taught in the New Testament in 2nd Corinthians chapter 9 verse 6-7: 'But this I say, He which soweth sparingly shall reap also sparingly; and he which soweth bountifully shall reap also bountifully. Every man according as he purposeth in his heart, so let him give; not grudgingly, or of necessity: for God loveth a cheerful giver'. The Lord Jesus also taught that it was 'more blessed to give than to receive,' Acts 20. 35. I think on the basis of these verses it would be unwise to charge interest if lending personally to family or fellow believers.

Helping the Poor – Giving

One of the things a believer should be known for is helping those who are disadvantaged or poor. In the early church preachers were expected not only to preach but to 'remember the poor' - in other words they would tell them about the Lord and salvation but show them kindness as well. In 2nd Corinthians chapter 8 and 9 Paul encourages the church in Corinth to remember the poor believers in Judaea just as the churches of Macedonia had done. It is obvious from these references that believers in the early church used their money to help other believers and non-Christians at times, Gal. 6. 10.

Helping the Poor – Lending

In Deuteronomy chapter 15 Moses teaches the people to be generous when giving to the poor. But in verse 8 he says, 'open your hand wide unto him' and 'lend him sufficient for his need'. There are many conditions that are attached to this type of lending (Deut. 24. 6-15, Exod. 22. 25-27) to make sure that poor people are not disadvantaged or manipulated for profit. These principles can be applied in our society as well.

We have two more issues to discuss in this chapter, gambling, and direct share ownership.

Before I talk about shares in general (and the sin of gambling) let me briefly highlight a situation that arose mainly in the late 20th and early 21st century.

In 1956 San Fransisco lawyer and economist Louis O. Kelso created the first employee stock ownership plan (ESOP) as a way of moving ownership of Peninsula Newspapers, Inc. from its two founders (both then in their 80s) to their chosen successors, the managers and employees. This method of remuneration did not really take off until the 1970s. It then became quite commonplace for companies to pay their employees some of their remuneration in either shares or share options. It is not within my remit to discuss the merits of this method of remuneration but ask and seek to answer the question – What should a Christian do if offered shares or share options? The scripture teaches that 'the labourer is worthy of his hire,' Luke 10. 7. On this basis I am persuaded that there is nothing wrong in accepting this form of payment if it fits with your financial situation.

Gambling and Share Ownership

Some people think that gambling and share ownership are the same thing. Depending on what shares you are investing in, this could be the case. There is however a danger that is common to both gambling and share ownership - the danger of greed and covetousness. The Bible warns against greed and covetousness in Exodus 20:15, 17; 1 Corinthians 6:9-10; and Colossians 3:5. Scripture makes it clear that a Christian man or women should earn their living by doing a good day's work. This principle means we should not rely on chance to create income, 2 Thess. 3. 10-12. In 1st Thessalonians chapter 5 verse 22 we read: 'abstain from all appearance of evil'. Gambling has damaged many people's lives by causing them to lose money that could have been used for good purposes or to cover day to day living costs. What God has given us should be used for good purposes and not evil. Anyone who wants to please God should not be involved in gambling.

Billy Graham, the renowned evangelist, once said, 'Gambling is also wrong because of the motives involved. Some people gamble for thrills and excitement. Others gamble because they have a greedy and covetous attitude about money. Some gamble out of a false belief in luck. All of these motives are wrong for the Christian, for they are all self-centered and materialistic.'

Motives for investing

In all areas of life which involve money we need to be careful about our motives and be wise about how we use our money. If someone is buying shares without knowledge of the market they are investing in and are recklessly seeking to make a quick profit they would be wise to resist the temptation. Many investors spend hours looking at the businesses they are considering investing in and seek to act prudently and cautiously in their investment strategy. At the end of the day a believer needs to behave as their conscience demands when deciding about share ownership. Their conscience should be clear, and they should be able to say in the words of James 4. 15: 'if the Lord will, we shall live, and do this, or that'. This is a good maxim for Christian living and decision making.

THE MONEY MAZE

CHAPTER 7
GETTING WHAT YOU WANT OR NEED - SPENDING MONEY

> *'Never spend your money before you have earned it.'*
> *Thomas Jefferson*

> *'Delight yourself in the LORD, and he will give you the desires of your heart.' Psalm 37.4, ESV*

The basic question we are answering in this chapter is - Is it wrong to enjoy yourself or to spend money? Should you feel guilty when you do something nice or have a thrilling experience?

Let me answer this very simply - No. There is nothing in the Bible that teaches these things. We were created with the ability to appreciate beauty and to experience pleasure. It is recorded in Genesis chapter one that when God made the world, He repeatedly saw 'it was good'. He appreciated the beauty, order, and splendour of the uncontaminated world that He had created. As the creation account proceeds, we see God make a help meet for Adam. Adam and his new wife must have been very beautiful and fully enjoyed all the pleasure of living in a perfect world. In these early days of creation, they experienced and appreciated a wonderful relationship which included sexual pleasure and intimacy. They were designed to fulfil each other and be the best of mates socially, sexually, intellectually, and emotionally. The account of 'the fall' and the entrance of sin into the world is against the background of a world where the food was not only nutritious but aesthetically appealing, Gen. 3. 6. I am sure that there were other trees in the garden that provided tasty and attractive food but there was something very appealing about the tree of the knowledge of good and evil. Eve saw that the tree was not only good for food but 'a tree to be desired to make one wise'. My point - there is nothing in this passage that indicates that there was a problem with good food, attractive things, knowledge, or wisdom. The issue was that the serpent, the Devil in disguise, Rev. 12. 9, was suggesting that God was depriving them and that their way, and the Devil's way, of disobedience would produce better results.

Nothing much has changed. The pleasures that the world offers and route to satisfaction that it suggests is selfish and self-centred and in the long run distances us from God. Whereas the joy that God offers is centred in Him, unselfish in its focus and ultimately is for our pleasure.

Firstly, let's look at one illustration from the life and experience of the Lord Jesus when He was living on earth. In John chapter 2 He attended a wedding and brought blessing to all the guests. The wine had run out and the Lord Jesus turned water into wine. Alcohol is damaging if drunk to excess and many Christians believe that, although there is not a direct prohibition on drinking alcohol in the Bible, men and women who want to live dedicated lives for God abstain from drinking alcohol, see Numbers 6 etc. Wine, however, is often used to describe the joy and gladness that people look for in life, Psalm 104. 15, and I think the lesson in this story from the Gospels is that the ultimate joy even in the happiest of events i.e., a wedding, will come from what the Lord Jesus offers.

I have just referred to Psalm 104. That particular psalm describes the many practical things God has done to make life pleasant for people. The examples include enjoying the physical creation (countryside and natural beauty), the refreshment of springs, streams and rivers, the fertility of the earth to produce good crops for food and olive oil to smooth the skin. It culminates with a shout of praise in verse 24: 'O LORD, what a variety of things you have made!' NLT.

I am going to resist giving more examples. The scripture is full of examples of the generous provision of God for His creatures' blessing and comfort. But what of heaven? When we have finished life on earth there is the prospect of heaven for all who have repented and believed the gospel. What is heaven like? Psalm 16 verse 11 says: 'You make known to me the path of life; in your presence there is fullness of joy; at your right hand are pleasures forevermore,' ESV. Heaven is a place of joy and pleasure. There are many other references like this - no tears, no separation, no death, and so on.

It is therefore clear that God is not against pleasure, joy, satisfaction, delight and all the things we so clearly desire, but the question is: Can we enjoy them without Him? Are our desires just for our own selfish pleasure? Where does desire stop, and covetousness start? How do I know when I'm actually being greedy?

You see, our fallen nature and sin have warped us so that what we think will satisfy us, doesn't! Our idea of pleasure is often not accurate and is not for our good. It is a problem that only God can solve.

In the book of Ecclesiastes, King Solomon pursues every form of pleasure that was available to him. Read the book for yourself, it

> **There is nothing wrong with pleasure, but it will never satisfy you without God."**

is only twelve chapters, it won't take you long. Solomon thinks spending money will make him happy. He was in the fortunate position of being extremely wealthy, but he soon discovers it doesn't make him happy. He tried everything - comedy and laughter, wine and wisdom, building projects, gardens, orchards, lakes and water features, fully-staffed country houses, buying collectors' items and museum pieces, private choirs, orchestras, intellectual debates and study - everything, but at end of the day he says, 'this is also vanity'. The advice of Solomon, the wisest man who ever lived, was this - you need truth, Ecc. 12. 10, you need wisdom and a shepherd (someone to care), 12. 11, you need to respect and honour God and obey Him, 12. 13, 14.

There is nothing wrong with pleasure, but it will never satisfy you without God. As I conclude this chapter, please turn in your Bible to Psalm 37. This Psalm and Psalm 73 were written when David and Asaph, who wrote Psalm 73, were frustrated that evil people seemed to get away without problems and were getting rich and prospering. I want to look at verse 4:

'Delight yourself also in the LORD, and He shall give you the desires of your heart,' NKJV.

Is it wrong to want good things in life? - No. Are there better things to set your heart on? - Yes. Colossians chapter 3 verses 1-4 make that clear. But how do I make sure that I want the right things in life. Focus on the Lord, focus on heaven, Col. 3. 2. If you delight in the Lord, then you will want what He wants, you'll begin to think as He thinks, and His desires will become your desires. He will give you the desires of your heart. I think this is a great formula for being satisfied and content in life.

God may give you a good life, but He may have lessons to teach you in bad times as well. He is working in your life and testing you to develop your faith, 1 Peter 1. 7. Money could fuel your greed but, as we learned in an earlier chapter, it is 'the love of money' that is the root of all evil. Waiting on God and trusting Him will make you more patient so in the words of James chapter 1 verse 4: 'Let patience have her perfect work, that ye may be perfect and entire, wanting - nothing'.

This is an important issue for all Christians to get to grips with in their journey to heaven - thanks for reading this chapter.

THE MONEY MAZE

CHAPTER 8
GIVING TO GOD, HIS WORK, AND HIS WORKERS.

> *'Don't expect to receive if you're not willing to give.'*
> *Anonymous*

> *'God loves a cheerful giver.'* - 2 Corinthians 9.7, NKJV

Different parts of the world have different attitudes to money. In the United Kingdom, where I live, you would never ask someone how much they spent on their daughter's wedding or how much their car cost. However, people from other cultures don't have the same reticence about money as I discovered when a brother asked me how much I had spent on my daughter's wedding. Shock, horror - you just don't ask those questions.

Another 'no go' area I have discovered is that men and women who serve God and live by faith, depending on Him for their income, don't talk about money. So, here am I writing a book about money! Which is OK, I think, as I am looking at what the Bible teaches about the subject and not merely telling you my opinion. But we need to be honest and accept that writers and speakers find it very hard to be completely unbiased when talking about certain topics. So, I need to tread carefully in this chapter. I serve God and my income comes from Him though local churches and individuals as the Lord lays it on their hearts.

What are my obligations to God when it comes to money & tithing?

I think we have answered the first part of the question in a number of the previous chapters as it is part of my reason for writing this book to warn (and be warned) about the Christian's relationship to money and conversely how money can be used for the glory of God.

So, what about tithing? The word 'tithe' means 'to give a tenth part'. The first time that we read the word is in Genesis chapter 28 verse 22. Jacob had been bargaining with God, which is not really a good thing to do. He told God that if He, God, stays with him, feeds, and clothes him and brings him back home to his father's house that one of the things he will do is give God ten percent of all that God gives him. He is saying to God: "If You prosper me, I will give You ten percent back. At this stage there was no law that said he had to do this, but he made this promise.

When Moses was writing the law of God for the second time in Deuteronomy, he states that a Jewish citizen had a legal obligation to give ten percent of their annual profits to the Lord God, Deut. 14. 22, 23. We get more details of this in Deuteronomy chapter 26. At the beginning of the harvest the Israelite was expected to bring to God their first fruits, i.e., they gave the first part of all their crops as an expression of gratitude to God. In verses 1-11 we see an individual coming and setting their basket full of produce before God. Because this person is grateful and delighted with what God has done for them, they are worshiping and thanking Him. Keep this idea of gratefulness, thankfulness, and worship in the back of your mind. We will come back to it.

In this passage, Deuteronomy 26, we discover that every third year they had to bring a second tithe. This was to be shared with those in need - the Levite, the stranger, the fatherless and the widow. Again, please store this principle of sharing what you have with those in need - we will need to revisit this before the end of this chapter.

There are many examples of giving that we could look at in the Old Testament. I am going to leave you to explore some of these for yourself. Think of the generosity of the people and what they gave in Exodus chapter 35 so that the Tabernacle could be constructed. Read the exciting account of King David giving from his personal wealth to build the first Jewish Temple in 1 Chronicles chapter 28. Consider the effect of this on others in chapter 29 as they added what they had to what was already an impressive pool of resources. God loves a cheerful giver, 2 Cor. 9. 7, and the Old Testament is rich with examples of such a spirit of generosity. The question really should not be: How much do I have to give? Or what is the minimum that I should give? But what can I give in light of all that the Lord has done for me?

The careful and sensible managing of charitable gifts is a topic which this book is not going address in any detail. In the passages that I have selected from the New Testament about giving you will see that it is important that trustworthy people are given the task of handing the funds that believers give from their 'hard earned cash', 2 Cor. 8. 16-24.

While the New Testament does not specifically instruct the believer to bring ten percent of their earnings, it is a good principle to work on, think of Jacob. We should bring to God the best of what we have, give Him first before spending on ourselves and have the same spirit of thankfulness and appreciation for His goodness and generosity to us as they clearly had in the Old Testament.

There are two main chapters in my mind that teach us the principles about giving for the Christian in the New Testament, 2 Corinthians 8 & 9. There are a number of other passages that make some reference to the subject, but we will restrict ourselves to these. Before we turn to them, let me remind you of a scene that the Lord Jesus described in the Gospel of Luke chapter 21. It is very relevant to our topic as it is about giving. The Lord Jesus sees rich men bringing their gifts to the temple treasury. I can just imagine the scene. They are strutting in, keen for everyone to notice them and making as big a scene as possible. 'Look at me' - 'I may be rich' - 'I give a lot to God' - 'I am so generous'. But, the Lord Jesus, just like His Father, God, sees everything. He sees everything in our lives as well and that's worth remembering.

Unnoticed, probably bent over and possibly shrunken with age an old lady creeps into the temple treasury. In the treasury there were large boxes for depositing the gifts and offerings. This poor lady is a widow. She has no husband and no source of income and as a result she would be desperately poor. But the Lord Jesus knows her heart and He is going to let everyone know how much He values her and her offering to God. Watch carefully as she drops her money in the box. Did you hear the chink of the coins? Probably not - it's only two small copper coins. Will it buy a seat in the temple? - no way. Will it feed a priest? Not even a mouthful! Does God value it? More than you could ever imagine.

What is the point of this incident being recorded in the scripture? You don't have to look far to find out. Listen again to the words of the Lord Jesus. 'Truly, I tell you, this poor widow has put in more than all of them,' verse 3, ESV. But you say - she only gave 'two small copper coins'. That's nothing! Keep listening. 'For they all (the rich men) contributed out of their abundance, but she out of her poverty put in all she had to live on,' verse 4, ESV. What is the Lord Jesus saying? He is telling us that these men had a lot more left where their money had come from. Their sacrifice was negligible. They had lots left. It is not that God doesn't value giving when the person who gives is rich; the point is that it doesn't cost the rich person as much to give as it does the poor person. You see, the poor widow gave everything she had.

Back to the question about how much should I give. Maybe the question should be: How much do I have left after I have given and then paid for all of my living costs?

This lesson is emphasized in 2 Corinthians 8 and 9. These are wonderful chapters that focus on the need for a local church to give to supply the needs of other believers who are in need. This is so relevant today as many in the body of Christ suffer through persecution or just the fact that they live in lesser developed countries. Could I ask you to read these two chapters and note the following points?

1. Giving by churches is an act of kindness for God, 8. 1.

2. It was poor Christians in poor churches who overflowed with generosity, 8. 2.

3. Giving generously has the added benefit of bringing joy to the giver, 8. 2.

4. Generous giving sometimes means going beyond what you thought was possible, 8. 3.

5. When you give genuinely you give yourself to God before you give your possessions, 8. 5.

6. Giving displays the grace of God in a Christian's life, 8. 6.

7. The Lord Jesus Christ is the highest example we have of giving, 8. 9.

8. Good intentions are not enough, you need to actually 'put your hand in your pocket,' 8. 11.

9. God does not expect you to give if you don't have the resources, 8. 12.

10. Giving is not meant to make life harder for you but to ease life for the other person by giving your surplus to meet their shortfall, 8. 13.

11. Giving is like sowing seed or making a good investment, the more you put in the more you will benefit - God will see you are never disadvantaged for giving, 2 Cor 9. 6. Please do not think this means your reward will be in money. It will be in a currency that is valuable in God's eyes, Matt. 6. 19-21.

12. You must do as you feel convinced in your heart. Do not give because you are under pressure, 2 Cor. 9. 7.

13. God will provide for your needs if you give for His pleasure and glory, 9. 8-14.

14. Be thankful for what God has given you and appreciate the indescribable gift of His Son and His salvation, 9. 15.

I am staggered as I complete this section at the wonder of God's Word not just in its detail and the practical guidance it gives but at the grace of God in my life.

> **... you [should] know where the money is going and how it will be used."**

How should I give?

Finally, for this chapter - how (not how much) should I give? This is really about the mechanics of giving i.e., through churches, Christian workers, charities etc. My advice will be brief as I have already given some hints in Chapter 2 and in Chapter 6.

From the passages we have been considering in 2 Corinthians and other New Testament writings my advice would be to give through local churches and Christian workers. This should mean that you know where the money is going and how it will be used. The intended effect is that gifts will be used to further spread the gospel and to establish new churches. Giving to support established assemblies of believers is also vital in developing parts of the world. In the Acts of the Apostles, as well as in 2nd Corinthians, we see that Christians had a social conscience and helped the poor and disadvantaged in society. While doing this with the ulterior motive of gaining converts would be wrong (and ineffective), Christians do believe that humanity's greatest need is spiritual and so everything we do should ultimately relate to our faith in the Lord Jesus.

Due to advanced banking and money payment systems sending money to individual Christian workers is relatively easy as is sending money to a local assembly if you know their bank details. Just be aware of the rates of exchange and additional fees that some apps or organizations apply. Ease of use sometimes costs money. There are a number of organizations that have been set up to facilitate sending money to churches and workers. Among the Christians I work with in the UK these are Lord's Work Trust and Echoes International. There are equivalent organizations in North America and other parts of the world. The benefit of sending your money through these service groups is that it will be tax efficient as they look after 'Gift Aid' and other government-approved schemes.

As I close this chapter my prayer is that the work of the Lord may prosper, and the Kingdom of God may increase as a result of the faithful and wise giving of God's people.

CHAPTER 9
THE PIGGY BANK IS EMPTY - BUDGETING AND PLANNING

> *'Failing to prepare is preparing to fail.'* - Benjamin Franklin

> *'Sit down first and count the cost.'* - Luke 14. 28, NKJV

I feel a little bit embarrassed talking about this particular topic. Why? Well, for many people this question is irrelevant. A significant proportion of the world's population is poor. They are like the widow we talked about in Chapter 8. In the line of the nursery rhyme, about Old Mother Hubbard looking for food, that many of us grew up with 'When she got there the cupboard was bare'. This is why the chapter on giving and tithing is so vital to read. If you haven't read it yet, please go back and do it now. When you have done this and know what you should do with your money then read this chapter about budgeting and planning.

The Bible is not a textbook on the practicalities of living but it does set out clear principles that we can apply to all areas of life. We have been thinking in this book about the believer's attitude to money. Hopefully by now you have worked out that the topic makes us think about a lot of other issues as well, some of them are listed below:

1. What we value in life.

2. What makes us passionate.

3. Jealousy and envy.

4. Fear, faith and trust.

5. Contentment.

6. Being earth focused or heaven focused.

7. Seeking God's will for my life.

8. Caring for others.

9. Selfishness or selflessness.

I have been challenged as I have thought and written about the topic. One of those challenges is to keep what the scriptures say about these various issues at the forefront of my mind and apply the principles I have discovered to my life.

In the remaining chapters of the book the one common question we ask is - Should a Christian plan for the future? Or put another way, does budgeting, planning, or saving for the future mean that I have a lack of faith and am not really trusting in God?

As we think about this, let me draw a picture for you. You have a good job and are able to pay all of your bills. You have money left over at the end of the week or month. You are getting on well and do not really have any worries about money (please do not stop reading if this is not the way things are for you - I will talk about you in a minute), so why would it be appropriate to have a budget and plan what you are going to spend and save?

Personally, I think it is always wise to plan whether you have limited or unlimited resources. The old adage: 'Failing to prepare is preparing to fail' by Benjamin Franklin, one of the founding fathers of the United States, is as true for money management as it is in other areas of life. In light of the teaching in Chapter 8, how will you know what you have available to help others or to give to the work of God if you do not do some planning? Most people, unless they are extremely disciplined and frugal, spend everything they have and then some more. This isn't necessarily correct or true for everyone but it's the way many people are. Therefore, it would be sensible, indeed wise, to sit down and prepare a simple income and expenditure plan. What do you have coming in? What are your fixed expenses? What can you afford to give to the Lord's work and to help others? Are you going to make a sacrifice so that you can give? Do you have other family or local church responsibilities that need to be considered? There are many things to consider and as a responsible believer you need to sit down and think these matters through.

As you think, jot down some possibilities. Do you need to replace your car? Will your local church need more money and support? Are you going to start a family at some stage or if you already have children what future expenses do you need to think about?

Is this just my hunch as an ex-banker or do the scriptures give us some guidelines? You will know if you have read the Bible for any length of time that God doesn't mince His words when stating truths. In God's eyes families are the bedrock of society and we, men in particular, have a responsibility to provide for our families. 1st Timothy chapter 5 verse 8 says: 'But if anyone does not provide for his own, and especially for those of his household, he has denied the faith and is worse than an unbeliever,' NKJV. So, this much is clear, we have a responsibility to provide so we had better be aware of what we earn and how much we have available to look after our families.

But there's more!

In Luke chapter 14 verses 25-33, the Lord Jesus is talking, to a crowd of people who followed Him, about the cost of being His disciple. He makes it clear that there is a price for following Him. Initially, He is not talking in terms of money (the cost could be the rejection of family and friends) but to illustrate His point the Lord talks about budgeting and planning for construction. You don't extend your home without getting some costings and working out if you can afford it in case you run out of money halfway through the job. It's a simple illustration that planning is a normal and prudent way to go about managing your finances.

In every area of our lives as believers we need to make our plans, and get on with life, but at the same time remember that the Lord is working out His purposes as well. I have mentioned James chapter 4 verse 15 before in this book. The lesson - make your plans but keep God in the picture, i.e., 'if the Lord will'. And don't plan with the determination that you will get your own way - be willing to accept the Lord's will if things don't happen as you planned. Remember the words of Psalm 37 verse 23: 'The steps of a good man are ordered by the LORD, and He delights in his way,' NKJV.

This principle will be emphasized again in the rest of the book.

CHAPTER 10
INSURING THE FUTURE - WISE OR OVERKILL?

> *'You don't buy life insurance because you are going to die, but because those you love are going to live.' Unknown Author*

> *'But if any provide not for his own, and especially for those of his own house, he hath denied the faith, and is worse than an infidel.' 1 Timothy 5:8*

There have been very godly believers who were convinced that they should trust God for everything and therefore insurance of any kind was out of the question. While I respect their views, but do not agree with them, I would be cautious about swinging too much to the other extreme.

I am not going to write a chapter defining the various types of insurance, as this would not be my area of expertise, so let me talk generally about insurance and then specifically about insuring your life. There are various terms for this, life insurance, term insurance, critical illness cover, health insurance and so on. The list is endless!

First of all, we have to accept that in certain countries certain forms of insurance are a legal requirement. So, for instance, it is illegal to drive a car in most countries if you do not have at least third-party car insurance cover. If you want to drive a car, you must insure it.

Secondly, most financial organizations will not lend you money to buy a house if you do not arrange life cover for the parties borrowing and house insurance to cover the property. They might even insist on critical illness and some form of health cover for the main income earner. You don't have a choice - if you want to borrow from them, then get insured. We have discussed in Chapter 5 about borrowing to get a place to live. If you are comfortable doing this then you will need to comply with the lender's conditions, one of which will be insurance cover.

Thirdly, most countries expect people to contribute to some form of health insurance. This might be publicly managed, such as the NHS in the United Kingdom, where you pay your National Insurance contribution directly from your income. Sadly, it's like tax, you never see it, as it comes off your pay before you receive the net amount. Many other countries have private health schemes but effectively they are similar arrangements.

These examples, in my mind, come under the teaching of Romans chapter 13 where we have a legal obligation to obey the law, to submit to the authorities, and to pay our taxes.

The question we are addressing is: Should a Christian insure themselves voluntarily? So, should you insure yourself in case you die, are terminally ill or are so incapacitated with illness that you cannot work? You will not be surprised to learn that there are no verses in scripture that address this question directly.

You could argue that an individual who is trusting God should just accept life as it comes and live with hardships and difficulties as they arise. It is a wonderful thing to be content and accept the circumstances of life as God sees fit to allow them. Paul could say in Philippians chapter 4 verse 11: 'For I have learned, in whatsoever state I am, therewith to be content'. In another passage (1 Tim. 6. 6-8) he states: 'But godliness with contentment is great gain. For we brought nothing into this world, and it is certain - we can carry nothing out. And having food and raiment let us be therewith content'. We must learn to be content when times are bad as much as we may feel content when times are good (I am sure you are aware that contentment is not guaranteed just because you have money in the bank - but that's another subject).

But does that mean that we do not plan and provide for the bad times? I think the record of Joseph in Egypt (Genesis 41. 46-57) would teach that preparing and planning for the bad times when we are in good times is wise and prudent. Hundreds of years ago your only option was to save money or produce like the farmer in Luke chapter 12 verses 16-21. Today, there are many financial products available to you to save carefully for days when things are more difficult. Insurance products are just one of the options that are available to you and they are designed to pay out when the difficult times come.

As you consider and decide what is the best course of action for you, please consider:

1. What you give to the Lord.

2. The help you can provide for the needy.

3. How content you are with what the Lord gives you.

4. That your trust should be in God not in your savings, 1 Tim. 6. 17.

What you must do is: 'Commit your works to the LORD, and your thoughts will be established', Proverbs 16. 3 NKJV, as all of our planning must take the Lord and His will into account.

Remember the words of Proverbs chapter 19 verse 21: 'There are many plans in a man's heart, nevertheless the LORD's counsel—that will stand,' NKJV. God wants us to be wise and careful. He expects, indeed He demands, that we look after our families and spouses and plan to provide for and protect them - and this includes looking at the differing possibilities that will face us in the pathway of life.

Let me close this chapter with a final quotation from Proverbs. You can see that 'the book of wisdom' helps us a lot on this topic. Proverbs chapter 21 verse 5 says: 'The plans of the diligent certainly lead to profit, but anyone who is reckless certainly becomes poor,' CSB.

Another set of proverbs, sorry I can't help it, they are so good -

'Trust in the LORD with all your heart, and lean not on your own understanding; In all your ways acknowledge Him, and He shall direct your paths. Do not be wise in your own eyes; Fear the LORD and depart from evil. It will be health to your flesh, and strength to your bones. Honour the LORD with your possessions, and with the firstfruits of all your increase; So your barns will be filled with plenty, and your vats will overflow with new wine', Proverbs 3. 5-10, NKJV.

CHAPTER 11

ENDING WELL - PLANNING FOR RETIREMENT

> *'The challenge of retirement is how to spend time without spending money.'* Author Unknown

> *'The plans of the diligent certainly lead to profit, but anyone who is reckless certainly becomes poor.'* Proverbs 21. 5, CSB

Most people would like to live to be old as long as they are fit and well and have a clear mind. Sadly, life is not always like that although people do seem to be living longer in certain parts of the world. If you retire in your 50s or 60s and live into your 80s then you have a significant part of your life to live when you are not earning. The answer to this in certain countries has been to raise the age of retirement, which for most people is not a great prospect. Imagine working into your seventies and eighties!

The subject of planning and the will of God for the Christian has been addressed a few times in recent chapters. Some of the issues relating to saving for the future and insurance as a form of saving have been covered in Chapter 3 and in Chapter 10 - so I am not going to revisit these topics again.

I would like to focus this chapter on trusting God in old age and ending well in your Christian life, the blessing of having an inheritance to pass on to the next generation and living with one eye open to the fact that the Lord Jesus could return in our lifetime. There are practical issues to consider when thinking about retirement and old age. I am going to throw them out for you to think about.

1. I am sure that you will still want to still be independent if you are physically fit and well, so how will you plan for this?

2. If you had to go into some type of care facility, how would you fund it?

3. If all of your assets are in your name and not shared legally between you, your spouse, and your family you may have to use all of your resources to fund a future care package. Think this one through carefully from an ethical and practical point of view.

4. Would you like to have something to leave to your children or is this a luxury you cannot afford?

5. Can you save now (and make a few sacrifices) to make things easier when income is lower, and you are not able to work?

Parents have a natural inclination to provide for their families. This is a biblical concept that was established in the Word of God. In 2 Corinthians chapter 12 verse 14 we read: 'The children ought not to lay up for the parents, but the parents for the children.' When considering widows and their needs the Apostle Paul writes in 1 Timothy chapter 5 verse 8 that the wider family should care and provide for those of their 'own house'. He also states that to fail to do so is a practical denial of the faith: 'But if any provide not for his own, and specially for those of his own house, he hath denied the faith, and is worse than an infidel.' These are important principles to bear in mind when thinking about the future, your planning strategies and how you as the retiree might want to prepare or you as a family member might be in a position to look after older relatives.

The value of your inheritance & having something to pass on to the next generation

I would like you to think of what you will leave your family in terms of a spiritual legacy as well as a financial one. Not everyone will be able to leave a significant financial legacy, but everyone can leave a rich spiritual legacy. Psalm chapter 37 verse 16 states: 'A little that a righteous man has is better than the riches of many wicked,' NKJV. God values spiritual things far more than material. The Psalm goes on to say in verse 18: 'The Lord knows the days of the upright, and their inheritance shall be for ever,' NKJV. I want to encourage you. You may not leave lots of money or property to your family, but you can leave them a godly example and share with them spiritual blessings that you have discovered in the person of the Lord Jesus. Aren't the words of Psalm 119 verse 72 so true: 'The law of your mouth is better to me than thousands of gold and silver pieces' ESV.

In light of all of the teaching that I have sought to present to you in this book, all that remains for me to say about saving and planning for retirement is:

1. It is not wrong to save and to plan, Prov. 21.5.

2. Be content with what you have and don't do anything out of a motive of greed, Heb. 13. 5.

3. Providing to ease the burden of others and to provide for your own family is a worthwhile objective, 2 Cor. 8. 13-15.

4. Seek the will of God before you make any decisions, James 4. 15.

5. Hold lightly to the things of this world and fix your focus on our soon coming Lord, Col. 3. 1-4, 2 Tim. 4. 6-8.

Should you write a will?

As with many of the topics addressed in this book, I cannot give you a 'chapter and verse' to answer this question. The idea of a 'last will and testament' is mentioned often in scripture. In Hebrews chapter 9 the writer explains that a will comes into force when the person who wrote it dies, Heb. 9. 16-17. This infers that it was a normal practice to leave instructions about how your legacy was to be handled when you died.

The first book of the Bible, Genesis, leaves ample evidence of how the Patriarchs passed on their legacy to the next generation. Many of these wills seem to have been 'oral wills' as the individual (Jacob for example in Genesis 48 and 49) gathered his immediate family around him to explain what was to be done upon his death. Jacob also gave instructions to Joseph about his burial arrangements.

In light of this it would be wise to have a will. It is also far safer, to avoid conflict, to have it in writing in a legally binding format.

CONCLUDING COMMENTS

My aim in this book has been to explain what the scriptures say about money and how that should be applied in everyday life. I hope you have enjoyed walking with me as we have chatted about money. It has been a longer journey than I expected it to be, but now I am going to leave you. Please make sure you pray as you process the information shared in this book, check the scripture references, and seek the will of God for your life in light of what you have discovered.

It might be useful to write down what you have learned as you read this book? Consider ways in which it has changed the way you think? Identify some of the hints that might be useful when helping and advising others who are asking the same questions.

Bear in mind that the way we think is affected by the mindset of the world round about us. So as believers, we need to rethink how we value money and its use. For instance, society often rates people according the size of their house, car etc. but as a Christian this is not appropriate. So, we need to teach each generation of new Christians how to avoid these pitfalls.

Also, false teaching will rear its ugly head from time to time. One of the current errors is the prosperity gospel. It is not biblical and impacts not only on our view of money, but it undermines the grace of God and the work of the gospel. How we think about money and success will influence how we live for God and the focus we place on serving Him. I must stop but you can see that the subject of money raises many questions and I hope this book will give you a biblical set of principles that can be used to answer them.

May I take the opportunity of thanking you for reading this book. I would also like to thank Emmaus for encouraging me to write and for their patience with me as it has taken me a long time to complete it. Finally, I want to thank my wife, Carole, for her patience with me as I have spent many hours away from her in my office researching and writing this book. My prayer is that as a result of all these sacrifices this book might be of some help to you on your journey home to heaven.

Stephen G Baker

Bibliography - all references to books that have influenced my thinking have been identified in the text of this book. If there are any omissions it is purely an oversight and not intentional. I willingly admit that much of my thinking will have been informed and developed through listening to many Bible teachers and talking with a significant number of believers. I am grateful to them all for the help that they have been in my life.

All **scripture quotations** are from the KJV unless otherwise indicated.